AN EXALTATION OF TONGUES

AN EXALTATION OF
TONGUES

POEMS

PAUL FISHER

MoonPathPress

Copyright © 2017 Paul Fisher

All rights reserved. No part of this publication may be reproduced distributed or transmitted in any form or by any means whatsoever without written permission from the publisher, except in the case of brief excerpts for critical reviews and articles. All inquiries should be addressed to MoonPath Press.

Poetry
ISBN 978-1-936657-32-2

Cover art: *Still Life with Crows and Volcano*
an original painting by Paul Fisher

Author photo: Courtesy of Linda Fisher

Design: Tonya Namura using Gentium Basic

MoonPath Press is dedicated to publishing
the finest poets
of the U.S. Pacific Northwest.

MoonPath Press
PO Box 445
Tillamook, OR 97141

MoonPathPress@gmail.com

http://MoonPathPress.com

For Linda

Acknowledgments

I wish to thank the editors of the following journals in which some of these poems first appeared, sometimes in slightly different versions:

The Antioch Review: "Linguistics for Beginners"
Autumn Sky Poetry Daily: "The Kiln God"
The Centrifugal Eye: "Forewarned," "Petrified"
Cirque Journal: "Affogato," "Black Moon White Mountain," "Drome"
Clementine Unbound: "The Secret Lives of Birds"
Clover, A Literary Rag: "Cat & Mouse," "The Man in the Shapeshifter's Mirror," "Questions for the Journey"
Conch.es: "Absolution," "Dog Day Siesta," "Slam"
Crab Creek Review: "A Singularity"
Cutthroat: a Journal of the Arts: "The Salt Wife"
Innisfree Poetry Journal: "Local Idiom"
Poetry on Busses, 4Culture: "Flow"
Umbrella Journal: "Midnight in the Garden"
Waccamaw Journal: "Jonah"
Wordwrights: "Domestication"

Contents

Linguistics for Beginners	3
Firebird	4
Hope	5
Midnight in the Garden	6
Jonah	7
Self-Portrait as a Sea Monster Contemplating the Moon	8
Flow	9
Garter Snakes	10
Petrified	11
Cat & Mouse	12
Drome	13
The Palomar	14
Necktie	15
The Dark Ages	16
A Question of Horizons	18
Local Idiom	20
Black Moon, White Mountain	21
Little Raven, Big Sun	22
Affogato	23
Developing Tray	24
Dog Day Siesta	25
The Kiln God	26
Happiness	27
Domestication	29

Old Dogs	30
Forewarned	31
The Secret Lives of Birds	32
Disappearing Ink	33
The Man in the Shapeshifter's Mirror	34
Toasts for an Undetermined Occasion	35
Absolution	36
Slam	37
The Salt Wife	38
A Singularity	39
About the Author	41

Every word was once a poem.
—Ralph Waldo Emerson

*Some words will never leave God's mouth,
no matter how hard you listen.*
—Mary Oliver

AN EXALTATION OF
TONGUES

Linguistics for Beginners

Break bread with silence.
Dish up the past.
Ask words to remember
the howl and hiss,
lips that authored fire,
the mouth which bore a kiss.

Let them tell you
as you stammer them out,
where they grew up
and how they got fat.

Inflate them with breath.
Throw your voice.
No sounds bounce down
the same canyon twice.

Face to face with the barrel
of a pen, they confess
to spells cast, miracles hooked,
everything inked,
from the green blood of grass
to the moon's missing half.

Are words enough?
Give them an ear.
They never shut up.

Written on skin or spoken by dust,
they recall when they meant
something utterly else,
and why even severed tongues
talk to themselves.

Firebird

Say it was a murder of crows,
a boil of hawks or a cloud of bats
that ripped the words
by their half-formed roots
from your still unbroken mouth.

Admit your wounded throat
made long and fearful sounds,
strings to stitch and hold your tongue,
splints to stop your tongue from wagging
like an almost severed tail.

Know your claustrophobic cries
lie buried under boards,
that what keeps pounding on your floor
is not some fleshless fist.

Never doubt that creatures
clawing up through dirt
or reaching up from breathless waters
ascend from childhood's tomb.

Mean it when you say
howling shapes your sky.
Strike the rock. Uncork springs.
Make caws and cackles fly from dreams.
Let your phoenix sing.

Hope

Impatient to be borne aloft
where thousands fly as one,
starlings roost in trees
the way words rest on tongues.
Given silence, night speaks.
Given light, wings beat.
A single quill inks the sky.
A million plumes define the sun.

With the din of darkness muted,
fire's fanfare hushed,
will song assume the form
of catbird, loon or meadowlark?
To rise from ash and ride on air
feathers must be strong.
Look where they have fallen.
Imagine where they have flown.

Midnight in the Garden

In this as yet undreamed-of tale,
I am not bilingual. Half your dying
language proves enough.

But you might ask me
why I then wear sheaths of stars
around the pale blue teardrop
of my back-lit pearl?

So I argue for the other side,
swallow words, shed my tail.
I teach my golden tongue to fork
before it greets two perfect strangers
free to quarrel, even as we speak,

over who will gather, who will hunt,
and who will sow, hands black with ink,
the blood-dark maize and bulgur wheat
in this as yet un-costumed tale.

Jonah

The whale welcomed me,
tongue meadow-rough, glossy
grin encompassing oceans,
black hole swallowing
promises, memory, gods.
O monstrous belly,
what alchemy occurred
before you spit my half-
digested self,
bone, blood, phlegm and shit
transformed, somewhere
among the galaxies,
without rudder, sail or oar,
between septillion stars, one life-
line spun from prayer?

Self-Portrait as a Sea Monster Contemplating the Moon
After the painting by Tom Nakashima

Poor moon, to find yourself
painted into the corner
of a Japanese byobu screen.
You can't know who levitated you
above my saw-toothed ocean
whose waves, poised at their peak,
have stood so long they've forgotten
they were born to break.

Do you look down with envy
as I ogle you in awe?
Do you feel the heat of serpent eyes
and hear the hiss of lava
as it sears its way toward heaven,
then splashes down to earth
like every other bit of ash
or fiery ball of wings and wax?

I would tell you I'm transfixed
by the play of light on skin,
that I'm frozen in the beacon
of your unrelenting stare.
But silence is my seamstress.
She measures me for scales,
clips my claws, gloves my hands,
and binds my singing tongue.

Flow

Be water my friend.
—Bruce Lee

Because you're water,
rain offers you words.
Because you breathe,
sea deepens your voice
with torrents and tongues
unheard since the flood.
Because you are the ocean you fill,
you must stir your own mud
and cast your own spell.

Garter Snakes

Curled in a nave of the garden,
    born live in ruins of the choir,
how lucky are her young,
    how blessed.

In the quarry they slip
    between stones, whisper
in tracery tongues
    cool and ancient as moss.

They wake to the first
    or final kiss of whatever wisp
leans over their nest.
    From half-closed fists

they stare with eyes almost
    like ours. We see their hunger,
moist as a tendril,
    unfurl toward frail light.

How eager they appear
    in coils of their mother
to swallow whole
    our cloudless weather

where blood, innocent as lightning
    and cold as any stream
within the mountains or the mind,
    beckons with its still, small voice.

Petrified

Around her circle ravenous gulls,
    bone of a moon, red—
shifting stars. Wind and rain
    erode copper hair. Sleet pocks
once translucent skin.
    While horse, deer and fox
lick salt from her feet,
    she dreams day and night
of houses aflame,
    of blizzard-thick ash
swaddling her grief.
    Were it possible to speak,
conceivable to wake, what then?
    She cannot quiet salacious crows,
quench mineral tears,
    roll stones from dead tongues.
The moment she blinked,
    scuttling leaves froze.
When she was a girl,
    when she was a wife,
when she played trick-or-treat,
    when she turned for a last
quick glance at her life . . .

Cat & Mouse

As my little cat toys
with his captured mouse,
a question mark flails
from the bars of his jaws.

I know he bears no malice,
that all of nature kills,
yet I think of *Tom & Jerry*,
of *Mighty Mouse* cartoons,
and of the latest plague of rodents
nibbling at the moon.

I think of Noah calking his ark,
the neigh, bray, yawp and snort,
a hubbub of hammers,
a yammer of tongues,
a scurry of tails and toes.

I hear Yahweh laughing
from his cockscomb cloud
because he knows the nanosecond
that cacophonous belly will close.

Drome
> *God moves in a long 'o'.*
> —Dylan Thomas

Sound the gong older than stars.
Hear the drumroll of engines revving.
Awaken your slumbering ears.

Inhale the echoes of beaten bronze bells.
Enlighten your ignorant throat.

Be the hair-shirted monk
in a crimson-clad dream.
Let *bone, grotto, obo, orange*
resound through your ten trillion cells.

Let dawn leak birdsong
between shutter slats. Let breezes
pass you unwritten notes.

Rise for a stroll through temples of sun
where brilliant staccatos of jackdaws and jays
instruct your stammering tongue.

The Palomar
*One of the last vaudeville theaters in America,
demolished in the 1960's to make room for
a post office and parking garage.*

At the age of six, I believed
the tuxedoed magician as he sawed
two naked legs—soon twenty feet
downstage and kicking—
from the screaming upper half
of his blindingly blond assistant.
I wept when on its own, each thigh,
ankle and tapping toe returned.

I believed I heard the memory man
rattle names of every soul
from box to balcony backwards.
I believed I saw the memory man's wink
turn to tongue, turn to whisper
in my mother's ear
the moment she shook his hand.

I believe the memory man's de facto
defunct, the Palomar's last act
was Sammy Davis Jr., and postal workers
will someday serve everyone in line
from drunks at Third and Union
to stiffs on Pike and Pine.

Necktie

Worn threadbare
from everyday use
and self abuse,
a silken noose,
a lifeline flung,
a choker passed
from father to son.

A top dog's whip,
an underdog's leash,
the flag unfurled
on a mannequin's shirt,
a pendulum
for an aging clock,
the airless corpse
of an old windsock,
a chain to yank,
a gift to fold—
best when paired
with a rubber nose.

A wagging tongue,
an unrolled scroll,
the tourniquet
for a hundred wounds,
the double cross
of a Windsor Knot,
breastplate, bib,
albatross.

The Dark Ages

During the dark ages
books were scarce
but phones were scarcer.
Reception sucked.
Static ruled.
Flat-Earthers lived in fear
of talking snakes
and tongue-tied kings.
Monks took vows of silence
yet couldn't hear the Word.

During the dark ages
bedbugs spread. War won.
Plague towns boomed.
Lincoln Logs and Legos
made fort building fun.
The moon, ringed with moths
and silly schoolgirls,
strained at its anchor chains,
warping the world.
Candle-lit haloes
hallowed the ground.
Too many sunsets
proved imagined fires real.

During the dark ages
rock & roll thrived.
Burgers were cheap.
Presidents lied.
When White Castle closed
I thumbed a ride home.

My mother, the queen,
introduced me to you.
The burning bush flared.
The dead rose from tombs.
In your cloudless eyes
The Renaissance bloomed.

A Question of Horizons

If we listen to the tangled wires
sparking in our brains,
we might conclude it's hard to read
the signs angelic fingers scratch
across chalkboards in our dreams.

Despite our best attempts
to introduce dead friends
at midnight's school reunions,
we might find it difficult to breathe
one letter of their names.

If we believe the prophets
blinded by their own illuminations,
or burned by lightning
prodding them to leap,
we might see heaven and hell
as flip-sides of pennies
flattened on imaginary rails
which bear the weight of real trains.

Drawn toward one vanishing point,
tracks might converge
in a mindscape tenderized by hail.
X might only mark the stubble,
that motherboard of brail
cold as an Iowa winter.

Impudent ice, our lascivious guest,
might invade every furrow
then disappear, leaving us to ask

what other tongues salted with sea
lick the roots of tallgrass prairie,
then soften to rain on Elysian Fields.

Local Idiom

Zigzag through nameless woods,
I scan my skies for chimney smoke.
Like beavers that trouble our pond,
I'm comfortable closer to home.
I gnaw only edges of worlds.
When I spit them out, they caulk my lodge
and drip from its cloud-stained dome.
Threadbare firs encircle me
like a nave of blue whale ribs
while wolves chew the full mead moon
down to opalescent bone.

But I was catching other dreams
at our camp by the cold crater's rim,
the night we skipped star-stones.
A fool for you, I tossed the crumpled
wings of this poem into our fire,
then kicked at its coals
with my bare, burning feet
till embers hissed, flared and sputtered out.
In the land of missed opportunity and stumps
where silence chants its lacquered prayer
and half the language gongs,
I ate our howling ashes—bitter in my belly,
yet sweet as stolen honey
ladled from the Great Bear's tongue.

Black Moon, White Mountain

An eclipse like a coin
dipped in ink
dares me to drink
from night's full cup.

The shadow I sip
quickens my brain
but darkens my tongue.
Penumbra and umbra
drip from my mouth.

My campfire wakes to lap
whatever wonder spills.
But cratered Kulshan sleeps
for now
on snowy haunches
hunkered down.

A distant howling thins
into sleepless strings of stars.

Above me, threads of cedar smoke
—sky's untiring magic ropes—
rise into the mystery
and vanish like a prayer.

Little Raven, Big Sun

Bomber to the core,
you have no need of laser sights
to crater streets with stolen nuts
or strafe coyote's kill.

Nothing keeps your backlit beak
from nailing me with spit-out pits
stripped of purple cherry flesh.
So what stops your bird-bright brain
from ravening after my remains?

Upstaging sun, you hurl a caw
out of the blue toward me.
Or is your tongue-slung missile aimed
to riddle all who crawl below?

Little eclipse, your halo's spiked.
You cock your dagger head
and spread your midnight wings.
A feather falls and a sunspot flares.
You're a fly in the eye of the photosphere.

Affogato

Glacier meets volcano
in the war between day and night.

No summer breeze or winter tease,
this shot's a jolt of fire and ice,

a vortex quick to drown itself
then sink into sleep again,

Yin and Yang making love in a bowl,
mountain and river flowing as one.

When you share its secret with your tongue,
you never eat alone.

Developing Tray

A thousand drops of rain
poised mid-burst on a pockmarked street
float beside firecrackers caught mid-crack
by an almost silent click.

In a sea shimmering black and white
the alchemy of space distills a spell
of sculpted smoke and flickering light.

Supernovas—time-bending roses
shrunk to the size of pre-engorged ticks—
swim beside close-ups of a rotting peach
which the sewer-sweetened tongues of critic mice
find good enough to eat.

Dog Day Siesta

Tepid dawn could not foretell
this air as thick as water,
this cannonball barrage of sun
stripping blond sky bare.

We pray for rain, imagine eclipse,
resign ourselves to half-lit dreams
where trumpet vine and ostrich fern
entangle us with shadow.

We submerge our sorrow
in untroubled ponds, cool our fear
in blue lagoons, and swallow the fire
of double-edged tongues.

We audition for the quietude
of atom, stone and star,
mute our horns, silence our drums,
and sleep like tired children,
our ears cocked toward the moon.

The Kiln God

Half-baked, he sits
on his blistering shelf,
naked and sizzling,
part demon, part elf.

No horns jut
from his hollow head,
but hissy-hot dreadlocks
snake from his scalp.

I turn up the gas
in my little brick kiln
till his stony grimace
outshines the sun.

He's unaware
that I gave him my eyes
and a tongue long enough
to catch butterflies.

Happiness

It knew my name
in its native tongue, a howl
heard by no one.

It broke the chain
that scarred its throat,
then jumped its fence, alone.

It had no lamp
but sniffed the dark. My scent
burned in its nostrils.

It cut through yards
till it reached night woods
lit only by an absent moon.

It ran through thorns
till it reached the sea
that hones the edge of the world.

It had no boat
but swam for its life
till it reached the cliffs of dawn.

It had no ladder
but scrambled up,
bleeding from its paws.

When at last we met,
in a dream I think, the beast
lay panting at my feet,

its well-gnawed bone of sorrow
clenched between my teeth.

Domestication

To make your wolf a dog,
you must wake before dawn.
All day you must grovel
on bleeding knees and paws.

You must have the patience
of a river-torn mountain,
knowing you will need
ten thousand dog generations.

You must sit, then heel.
And if you speak,
you must speak the tongue
of the bitch who suckled you.

Here is the leash. Here is the bone
etched by your father's teeth.
Good boy. Lie down. Sleep.

Old Dogs

When old dogs sing
to please new masters
or when they bite
their own unwieldy tongues,

when by instinct, by luck
or by the pounding
of their hungry hearts
old dogs escape from pens
but submit like pups
to the lure and the lick
of invisible bonds,

when sleeping bones ache
and old dogs wake,
do they glimpse for a moment
the wolf's wild stars?
Do they long for a taste
of the great mother's teats?

Do they find, sniffing ash
and wet-nosing grass,
the scent of her breath
beneath earth's wrinkled pelt?

Forewarned

The beverage you are about to enjoy
is hot. It's your right to slurp or sip,
but a crime to complain
with your burnt tongue and lip.

Women of childbearing age
are advised not to consume our product.
A significant number of test subjects
bore lizards, a smaller percentage
conceived gods.

Do not stand too close
to the edge of the platform.
We provide no railing, parachute or net.
If you desire wings, order in advance.
Allow a lifetime for delivery.

You must be five feet tall to ride.
Anyone shorter is sent to bed.
Anyone taller returns minus head.

The subway's lovely, dark and deep.
Its rats are fat as barnyard cats,
and the third rail's a hungry bitch.

Whatever you say or do
will be used against you.
If you cannot afford an attorney,
a baboon will be appointed.

Run for your life, but watch
where you walk. If nothing else, know
when to stop.

The Secret Lives of Birds

Snowy owls never read
the Annotated Guide to Birds,
but rooster feathers sometimes line
the nests of well-read hens.

Great white herons, unaware
of poems with ponds where they appear,
vanish like the dinosaurs they were
into the many minds of air.

Peopling the atmosphere
like winged seeds and unstrung kites,
cranes and egrets disappear
to emerge from mist as metaphor.

Birds like us go with the flow—
eagles high, wrens low.
With clipped wings and puffed up plumes,
parrot laureates hawk their tongues.

To learn what feathered brains know,
consult the raven, ask the crow.
Lose your phone. Fly alone.
Watch the harpy upchuck bones.

Disappearing Ink

Before planes crashed, before towers fell,
before Saint Helens blew heaven to hell,
before Atlanta burned on the screen,
before Atlantis circled the drain,
before Xanadu was an opium dream,
before appaloosas ran bridled and tame,
before Adam met Eve,
before love meant ice cream,
before eagle and wren divided the sky,
before sparrow and hawk taught humans to fly,
before Darwin's tortoise defined turtle soup,
before poets and writers emerged from swamps,
before Donald Trump out-quacked Donald Duck,
before word after word meant lie upon lie,
before shadows danced on sooty cave walls,
before starless ceilings eclipsed Santa Claus,
before Buddha died, before Jesus rose,
before mother tongues made rivers their roads,
before God issued *Aha* from Her lungs,
were signs of the times written on wind
before names were numbers scarred into skin?

The Man in the Shapeshifter's Mirror

Yesterday you were the bamboo boat
a poet drunk on dharma swore she saw
float off the page of a Sung dynasty scroll.
Today you are the engineer
aboard the longest coal train in the world.

Is this wailing wall of rusted cars
the clanking wheels of a chameleon like you,
or just a double-jointed dragon,
the origami lizard your reptile brain created?

Do doe-eyed cows whose names are bells
cast from molten bronze age gongs
announce themselves at Heaven's gate
as Kobe beef or filet mignon?

When your mother calls the hundredth time
to remind you she's deceased,
do you recognize the telltale rattle,
the plate tectonics of drowned prayer beads,
the voice ground smooth as a bone china vase?

How many times can you watch yourself
slip from a sheared sheep's skin,
then catch your breath
whetting the tongues of ravens and wolves
while singing a buffalo song?

If a washed-out trestle looms ahead,
will you be late?
Since crossing the bridge to nowhere
takes time, should you open the throttle
or hit the brakes?

Toasts for an Undetermined Occasion

1

To my left leg,
which is shorter than my right:
Because you bore my wobble and weight,
I learned to lean on you.

2

To my teeth,
never mistaken for ivory keys,
plastic fangs or spit-polished pearls:
You and my tongue have fallen in love.

3

To my eyes,
which often quarrel with each other:
Two visions sometimes
see farther than one.

4

To my skin of many colors:
I've memorized your well-rhymed scars,
and often walk the streets of sleep
deciphering your tight-lipped wounds.

Absolution

Forgive me if I bristle
as shadows climb the walls,
and voices from another room
repeat the words
our tongues once owned.

Forgive me as you did
the night our clock ran down,
and in the dark we found
the timeless beat of silence
without a metronome.

Forgive me if my hailstones
ping pong through the house
then clatter down dry canyons
to ice the buried fires
burning without sound.

Hear me when I say,
Through our electric skin
a sacred current flows.
Lightning fills our lungs
to clear our skies for songs.

Slam

Even when we read in silence
the throat's deep well
ripples like a spring-fed pool.
The tongue will not hold still.

Do shouted words ring true?
Ask the deafened air.

Ignore the buzz and blare
of restless skies and noisy stars.
To ease the ache between your ears
let the darkness hum to you.

The Salt Wife

Deer have long since licked
her weathered totem away,
even the slender fingers
she loved to slide through his hair.
Not bones but a brash tang of sea
is what remains of her
who refused to savor smoke
yet dared to taste the fire.

Not her lips, her breasts
or her crystalline skin,
but the ceaseless flow of her song . . .
You can hear it in the wind.
Or is it the man himself who sighs
because he too, in love with the world
devoured by tongues,
must share his bed with ghosts?

A Singularity

The moon behind the windsock
woke me: the hour, the elms,
the dancer in the light,
a shadow like an auspice
squirming on the wall.

Not the cat's rough tongue,
your kiss, our silly song,
just the moon behind the windsock,
the last act of the night,
a bow, a curtain call,
a blue and crimson wide-mouthed koi
performing for a cold blind eye.

The moon behind the windsock
woke me. My own black ink
must draw me
down to earth again.

About the Author

Paul Fisher was born and raised in Seattle where he currently lives with his wife, Linda, and where his grandfather, an immigrant from eastern Europe, settled in 1904. Because of economic necessity and a desire to broaden his horizons, Paul has lived and worked in more places around the country than he cares to think about. As a result, though he loves the Pacific Northwest, and its rugged landscapes haunt his dreams, his sense of place has expanded like space to include a multitude of universes.

The first member of his family to graduate from high school, let alone college, Paul earned a BA in Visual Arts, an MA in Arts and Education and, in 2005, an MFA in Poetry from New England College. In addition to teaching in and directing high school art programs for fifteen years, he has been employed as an environmental activist for Greenpeace, a llama wrangler on a ranch in the Columbia River Gorge, a chauffeur for the Eugene O'Neill Theater Center in Waterford, CT, an armed bank guard, a department store detective, and as a manager in an assisted living facility. Being a poet, artist, husband, father, grandfather and dog-cat-and-baby sitter are among the many things he does out of love. An unrepentant lefthander, he prefers tapping keyboards to pushing pens.

Paul is the recipient of an Individual Artist Fellowship in Poetry from the Oregon Arts Commission. His first Book, *Rumors of Shore*, won the 2009 Blue Light Book Award, and was published in 2010. His poems have appeared in journals, including *The Antioch Review, Cave Wall, The Centrifugal Eye, Crab Creek Review, Cutthroat, The Ekphrastic Review, Naugatuck River Review, Nimrod, Pedestal, Sow's Ear, Switched-on Gutenberg,* and in the best-selling anthology, *River of Earth and Sky: Poems for the 21st Century*. Some of his visual art has been exhibited at the Lyme Art Association Gallery in Old Lyme, CT, the Craft Alliance Center for Art & Design in St. Louis, MO, and the Frye Art Museum in Seattle.

www.ingramcontent.com/pod-product-compliance
Lightning Source LLC
Chambersburg PA
CBHW021452080526
44588CB00009B/818